AMERICAN CARS

THROUGH THE DECADES

American Cars of the 1960s

GR·RRR!

Craig Cheetham

GARETH STEVENS
GS
PUBLISHING
A Member of the WRC Media Family of Companies

Please visit our web site at: www.garethstevens.com
For a free color catalog describing Gareth Stevens Publishing's
list of high-quality books and multimedia programs,
call 1-800-542-2595 (USA) or 1-800-387-3178 (Canada).
Gareth Stevens Publishing's fax: (414) 332-3567.

Library of Congress Cataloging-in-Publication Data

Cheetham, Craig.
    American cars of the 1960s / Craig Cheetham.
        p. cm. — (American cars through the decades)
    Includes bibliographical references and index.
    ISBN-13: 978-0-8368-7725-0 (lib. bdg.)
    1. Automobiles—United States—History. I. Title.
TL23.C4415   2007
329.2220973'09046—dc22   2006051058

This North American edition first published in 2007 by
Gareth Stevens Publishing
A Member of the WRC Media Family of Companies
330 West Olive Street, Suite 100
Milwaukee, WI 53212 USA

Copyright © 2007 Amber Books Ltd

Produced by Amber Books Ltd., Bradley's Close,
74–77 White Lion Street, London N1 9PF, U.K.

Project Editor: Michael Spilling
Design: Joe Conneally

Gareth Stevens managing editor: Valerie J. Weber
Gareth Stevens editor: Alan Wachtel
Gareth Stevens art direction: Tammy West
Gareth Stevens cover design: Dave Kowalski
Gareth Stevens production: Jessica Yanke and Robert Kraus

Illustrations and photographs copyright International Masters
Publishers AB/Aerospace–Art-Tech

Printed in the United States of America

1 2 3 4 5 6 7 8 9 10 10 09 08 07 06

Table of Contents

Buick Riviera Grand Sport

Buick's luxury coupe — the Riviera Grand Sport — was a large, comfortable, expensive car.

Inside, the dashboard was wooden with chrome-ringed dials.

The Riviera had a huge **V-8** engine — 401 cubic inches (6,571 cubic centimeters).

The back end of the Riviera had panels that curved inward like the front end of a boat.

The Riviera's body was flatter than many other cars of the time, which had smooth, curvy lines.

The Riviera was one of the first American cars to have marker lights on each corner. These lights helped other drivers to see its exact position on the road.

The Riviera had a very long hood to house its large V-8 engine.

1963

Buick introduces the first Riviera. It has a four-headlight front end and a low roof.

1963

The company offers the "Grand Sport package" for the Riviera by fitting it with a 425-cubic-inch (6,965-cc) engine.

engine made 325 **horsepower**. The car could cruise easily at 100 miles (161 kilometers) per hour. The Grand Sport models were the top models in the Buick line.

B y the end of the 1950s, fins and chrome were no longer popular. In the 1960s, car makers looked for new shapes for cars.

Top of the Line

The Buick Riviera Grand Sport was one of the most stylish cars on the road. Buick designed the car for single people rather than families. The Riviera had a luxury interior and a flat-edged body — a look based on European coupes of the time. Its 401-cubic-inch (6,571-cc) V-8

UNDER THE SKIN

The Riviera was one of the first American cars not to have a separate **chassis**. All of its parts were bolted onto the car's body frame.

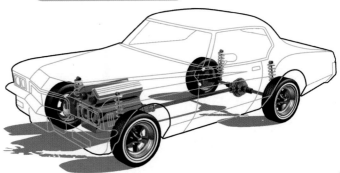

5

Checker A11 Cab

The Checker A11 taxi cab was so tough and reliable that it was made for more than twenty years.

The car's back door was wide and square, which made it easy for passengers to get in and out.

Passengers in Checker cabs usually had a bumpy ride. Its **suspension** was designed to last a long time, but the car was not comfortable.

The passenger cabin was large. As well as the back seat, the cab also had two small seats that folded out from the front seats.

Inside, the Checker cab had a bulletproof glass divider between the front and back seats to protect the driver from attack.

The Checker cab was durable. Many of them were still being used in the 1990s.

1963

The Checker A11 makes its debut. Buyers could choose from a wide range of engines and colors.

1974

The company adds bigger bumpers to the Checker to meet new government rules.

The Checker A11 cab was launched in 1963. It soon became one of the best-known cars on the road.

The driver's seat was high, giving a good view of traffic on busy streets. Big fenders gave good protection. Checkers were built to last. They were not the most comfortable cars, but they rarely broke down.

Trusty Workhorse

New York's yellow taxi cabs — many of which were Checker A11s — are world-famous. But the Checker A11, better known as the Checker cab, was driven everywhere. Other states had blue, white, red, and even black Checker cabs. Checker used different engines, including Chevrolet and Ford eight-**cylinder** engines, for its cabs.

UNDER THE SKIN

A six-cylinder or an eight-cylinder engine powered the Checker cab. The car had coil-spring suspension, which made it bumpy to ride in.

Chevrolet Camaro Z28

The Chevrolet Camaro was General Motor's answer to the Ford Mustang. The Z28 was faster than earlier Camaros.

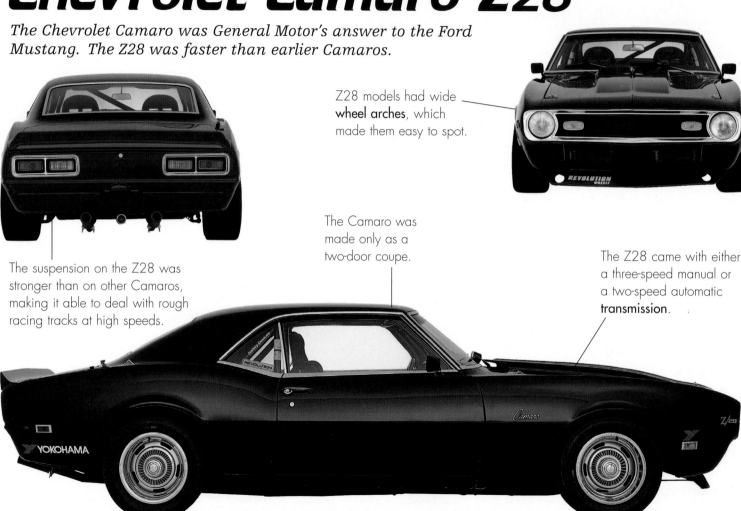

Z28 models had wide **wheel arches**, which made them easy to spot.

The suspension on the Z28 was stronger than on other Camaros, making it able to deal with rough racing tracks at high speeds.

The Camaro was made only as a two-door coupe.

The Z28 came with either a three-speed manual or a two-speed automatic **transmission**.

This Camaro Z28 has been painted in the blue paint and white stripes that are Chevrolet's racing colors.

1966

Chevrolet launches the first Camaro.

1967

The company introduces the Z28 Camaro (pictured below). It is the most powerful Camaro yet. Its power made it a successful racing car.

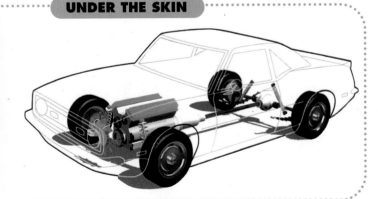

The Camaro was built to compete against Ford, which had sold more than one million Mustangs in its first year of production.

Road Racer

Chevrolet made several models of the Camaro, but the Z28 was the most powerful. It was designed for the Trans Am competition, a car race across the United States. Its 302-cubic-inch (4,949-cc) engine made over 300 horsepower. The car had a top speed of almost 130 miles (209 km) per hour and was popular with street racers. In 1968, it easily won the Trans Am championship. Driver Mark Donohue won ten of the race's thirteen rounds.

UNDER THE SKIN

The Z28 had shock absorbers to cope with tough track racing.

9

Chevrolet Corvette Sting Ray

The Sting Ray is a legend. It was the first American sports car that could go faster than the European models of the era.

The Sting Ray was made only as a coupe. It had a rear window made of two separate pieces of glass.

The Sting Ray had round taillights like the 1950s Corvette.

The Sting Ray was the first Corvette to feature pop-up headlights. Its headlights rose out of the hood, powered by electric motors.

Like all Corvettes, the Sting Ray's body was made out of **fiberglass**, so it never rusted.

The front fenders had three **vents** that forced air around the back of the engine to keep it from getting too hot.

10

The owner of this Sting Ray has added chrome wire wheels and tires with white bands.

MILESTONES

1963

The Sting Ray debuts. It is based on a racing car designed by General Motors's Bill Mitchell.

1967

The most powerful Sting Ray of all appears. It has a 427-cubic-inch (6,997-cc) **big-block engine**.

W hen Chevrolet introduced the Sting Ray in 1963, it was the fastest road car that any American company had ever built. It was Chevrolet's challenge to European makers such as Jaguar and Ferrari, whose cars many Americans were buying.

Besides selling well, the Sting Ray was popular on racetracks. It was driven by the winner of the Daytona 500 long-distance race in 1966.

Super Power

A 327-cubic-inch (5,359-cc) V-8 engine powered the Sting Ray. The car was light because of its fiberglass body. It was also fast, with a top speed of almost 150 miles (241 km) per hour.

UNDER THE SKIN

A tubular steel frame added strength to the Sting Ray's fiberglass body.

11

Dodge Charger 500

The 500 is the fastest, most powerful model of the famous Charger. It is one of the most prized muscle cars for collectors.

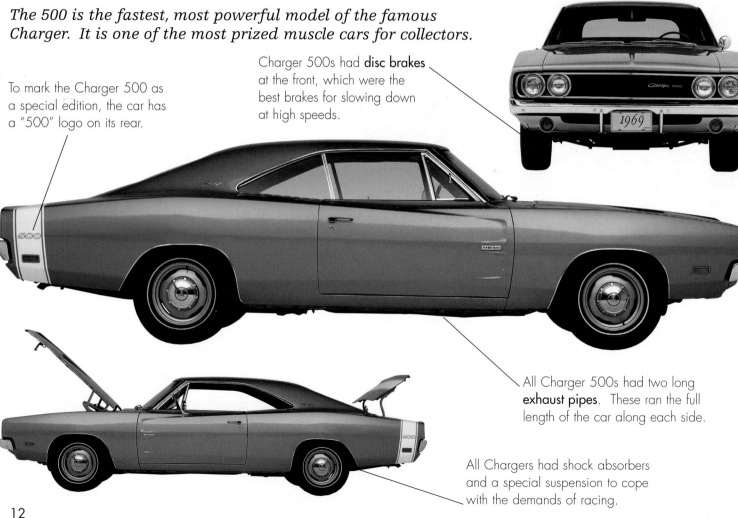

To mark the Charger 500 as a special edition, the car has a "500" logo on its rear.

Charger 500s had **disc brakes** at the front, which were the best brakes for slowing down at high speeds.

All Charger 500s had two long **exhaust pipes**. These ran the full length of the car along each side.

All Chargers had shock absorbers and a special suspension to cope with the demands of racing.

Some people compared the Charger's shape to a Coke bottle because the sides were slightly pinched in at the center, which made it look slightly curvy.

1967

The Charger appears as Dodge's first entry into the fast-growing muscle-car market.

1969

The Charger 500 wins eighteen NASCAR races in its second year on sale.

The Dodge Charger is best known today for its television and movie role as the "General Lee" in *The Dukes of Hazzard*. For most of the late 1960s, it was one of the most popular muscle cars in the United States.

Almost every car maker had a vehicle to compete in **stock car races**. For Dodge, it was the Charger 500, which was built in small numbers as a more powerful version of the Charger.

Racing Car

Zipping through the quarter mile in just 13.7 seconds, the Charger was also a successful racing car. In the 1960s, car dealers used to say "Win on Sunday, sell on Monday," which meant that success on the racetrack led to better sales in showrooms.

UNDER THE SKIN

The Charger 500 was a very powerful car. Its 440-cubic-inch (7,210-cc) engine put out 425 horsepower.

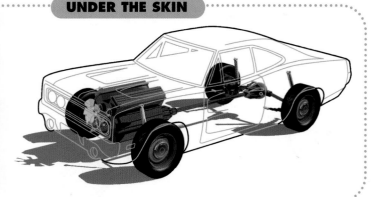

13

Ford Galaxie 500GL

The Galaxie was Ford's best-known NASCAR racer of the 1960s. It was both powerful and successful in races.

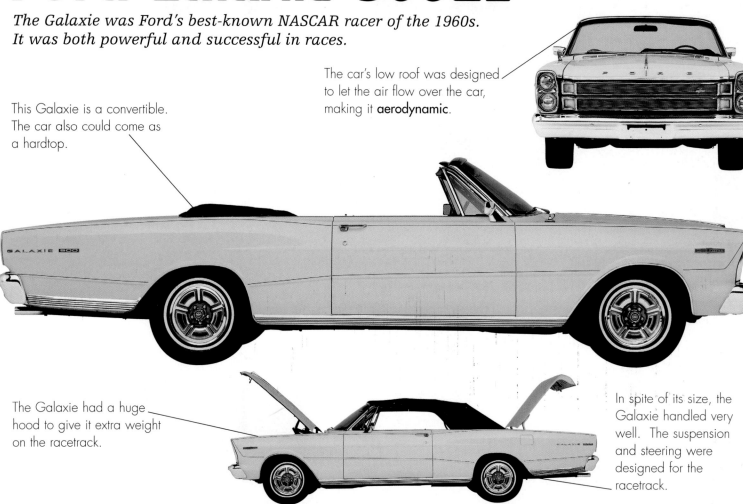

The car's low roof was designed to let the air flow over the car, making it **aerodynamic**.

This Galaxie is a convertible. The car also could come as a hardtop.

The Galaxie had a huge hood to give it extra weight on the racetrack.

In spite of its size, the Galaxie handled very well. The suspension and steering were designed for the racetrack.

14

This early Galaxie has stacked headlights, giving the hood a very square, powerful look.

1960

Ford's first-ever full-size sedan, the Galaxie, came both as a four-door model and as a two-door version called the "Fastback" (pictured below).

1965

The Galaxie's body is restyled to make it slimmer.

The Galaxie 500GL is one of the biggest cars that Ford ever built. Few people can forget the sight of it. It was designed both to be a popular family car and to compete in NASCAR races.

Track Champion

Even in the road models, it was easy to see this car was built for racing. The hood and trunk were oversize to give added protection when bumped on the racetrack. The low roof kept the car driving as smoothly as possible on the oval racetracks. The design worked. Not only did the car become a NASCAR champion, it also sold well as a street car.

UNDER THE SKIN

The body of the Galaxie was so big that even the biggest 427-cubic-inch (6,997-cc) engine looked small under its hood.

15

Ford Mustang 1966

When the Ford Mustang first arrived, its smooth, aggressive look caused quite a sensation. The car was soon very popular with young drivers.

The rear lights were three separate rectangular shapes. Mustangs still have this styling today.

The Mustang came with either a massive V-8 or a smaller six-cylinder engine.

Mustangs were famous for having side scoops, which were cut into each side of the body.

The Mustang came in three body styles: a two-door **sedan**, a two-door coupe, and a convertible with a power roof.

The Mustang featured here has been **customized.** The owner has made his own special model by painting the car bright orange and adding chrome wheels.

1961

Ford president Lee Iacocca decides Ford should make a sporty but cheap car.

1964

The Mustang goes on sale, and more than one million are sold before the end of the year.

W hen the Mustang first appeared, nobody imagined how successful it would be — not even Ford's bosses. The company's factory ended up running twenty-four hours a day during the first year of production just to keep up with orders. Ford sold more than one million Mustangs in the model's first year.

Success Story

The Mustang was such a success because Ford made versions of it that fitted different needs. The low-power, six-cylinder sedan was perfect for driving to work or to the mall. The race-tuned V-8 version was ideal for taking to the track on weekends.

UNDER THE SKIN

The Mustang looked modern, but it was a traditional car with a V-8 engine and four-speed **transmission.**

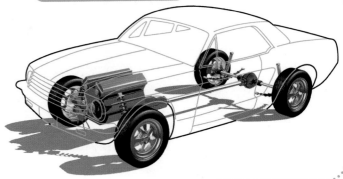

17

Mercury Cougar

The Cougar was somewhere between a muscle car and a cruiser. It looked stylish, and it had a very powerful engine.

Each of the car's forty slim red lights on the back had a separate lens cover.

The Mercury Cougar's headlights were hidden behind flaps that lifted up when a switch on the dashboard was flicked.

Like most muscle cars, the Cougar had a big engine under its hood — a 427-cubic-inch (6,997-cc) V-8.

The Cougar had chrome wheel rims.

With so much weight at its front, the Cougar was a difficult car to turn easily.

1967

Mercury introduces the Cougar, its first high-performance car.

1969

The Cougar gets a new look, with a bigger radiator **grille**.

Mercury knew that not everybody wanted to drive a muscle car. Mercury's owner, Ford, made the Mustang and the Galaxie, so Mercury wanted to try something different — the Cougar.

Powerful Elegance

The Cougar had the power of a muscle car, but its shape was less sporty. Its plain looks hid the fact that it was one of the most powerful cars of the 1960s. It had the same V-8 engine as the powerful Boss Mustang, which was the most powerful Mustang of the day. It could **accelerate** to 60 miles (96 km) per hour in just 7 seconds, and it had a top speed of 128 miles (206 km) per hour.

UNDER THE SKIN

Most of the Cougar's engine and suspension parts were the same as those in the Ford Mustang.

19

Oldsmobile 4-4-2

Oldsmobile entered the muscle car market with the 4-4-2. The company tried to make its muscle car different looking than others.

The convertible 4-4-2 had a power roof. Coupe versions were also available.

Some 4-4-2s had luxury gold-colored seats.

Many muscle cars have their wheels painted gold to make them more noticable.

The numbers "4-4-2" were written on the front sides of the car.

This 4-4-2 is a rare convertible model. Most 4-4-2s were two-door sedans.

1964

The name "4-4-2" is used by Oldsmobile for an extras package on its sedans.

1966

The name "4-4-2" is given to a new car in Oldsmobile's line.

Oldsmobile had never built muscle cars before, but the company wanted to sell cars to young people. Many young people in the 1960s wanted to drive muscle cars, so Oldsmobile built the 4-4-2.

powerful and could accelerate just as fast as its competitors, the 4-4-2 did not sell as well as other muscle cars of the time.

High Speed

The 4-4-2 soon became well-known for its power and speed. The 425-cubic-inch (6,965-cc) engine made the 4-4-2 as fast as the Ford Mustang and the Chevrolet Camaro Z28. Although its engine was

UNDER THE SKIN

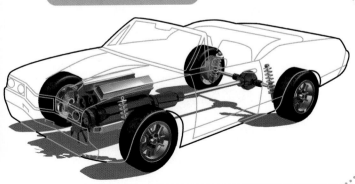

The 4-4-2 had good brakes that allowed it to stop quickly at high speeds. Its brakes were better than those of any other muscle cars of the time.

21

Oldsmobile Toronado

The Toronado did not sell well, but it was important because it was the first American car to have many features not seen before on the country's cars.

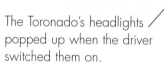

Oldsmobile gave the Toronado a sloping rear. The exhaust pipes poked through the chrome bumper.

The Toronado's headlights popped up when the driver switched them on.

The Toronado had **front-wheel drive**. This means that the engine powered the front wheels to make the car move.

The Toronado's front-wheel drive helped it grip the road better than most American cars of the time.

1966

General Motors launches its first front-wheel drive car, the Oldsmobile Toronado.

1971

The original Toronado is replaced by a redesigned model of the same name (pictured below).

The Toronado was one of the most important cars of the 1960s because it had a new kind of drive system.

world's cars. The Toronado was also set apart by its styling. Its headlights were hidden in pods, and its chrome bumpers and smooth sides combined American and European fashions.

Ground Breaker

It was the first American-made car with front-wheel drive. All other muscle cars had rear-wheel drive, but the Toronado's engine fed 385 horsepower to the front wheels. With no need to power the rear wheels, the car had a flat floor. This allowed space for up to six passengers. Not popular at first, this design is now used on more than 80 percent of the

UNDER THE SKIN

In the front-wheel drive layout, only the brakes need to be connected to the rear wheels.

23

Plymouth Roadrunner

Most muscle cars were expensive. Plymouth built the Roadrunner to appeal to muscle-car buyers who wanted to spend less money.

The Roadrunner looked plain, but its engine was very powerful.

The Roadrunner's hood was painted matte black in the center.

The car was named after the Roadrunner cartoon character. The outline of the famous Warner Brothers bird can be seen on the door.

Most Roadrunners had steel wheels.

The Roadrunner's wheels were painted to match the car's body color — in this case, wine red.

1968

Chrysler launches the Roadrunner and pays Warner Brothers $50,000 to use the same name as its famous cartoon character.

1970

Roadrunners get a redesigned front end (pictured below) and new taillights.

The Plymouth Roadrunner is one of the all-time great muscle cars. It was first built in 1968 after buyers asked for a cheaper car that could perform as well as a Dodge Charger, Pontiac GTO, or Ford Galaxie.

Simple Power

The Roadrunner was very simple inside and out. Modeled on the Plymouth Belvedere, it had vinyl trim, steel wheels, and a single color scheme all over. It was, however, very fast. Power came from the same 426-cubic-inch (6,981-cc) V-8 that Plymouth used in its NASCAR racers.

The Roadrunner's engine meant it could keep up with America's fastest street racers at a much cheaper price.

UNDER THE SKIN

The Roadrunner's chassis was based on an earlier Pymouth car, the Belvedere. The Belvedere had a simple, practical design.

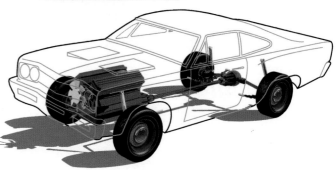

Plymouth Superbird

The Superbird looked unlike any other car on the road, but its unusual features were there for good reasons.

The big rear spoiler helped the air to press down the back of the car, which could lift at high speeds.

All Superbirds had vinyl tops. The vinyl, covered up rough metal. The metal was rough because the cars were built quickly.

Because the Superbird was built for racing, all versions came with a built-in **rollcage**.

The Superbird's nose was designed so that air flowed over it, forcing the body downward. This gave the front wheels more grip, helping them hold the road better at high speeds.

Plymouth

Superbirds came in many bright colors. Orange, lime green, yellow, and blue were popular.

By the late 1960s, most car makers in the United States believed that racing was important to help sell cars. Plymouth built the Superbird for the 1969 racing season. NASCAR's rules stated that a certain number of road cars had to be built before the model could be used for racing. As a result, the Superbird was rushed into production.

Superpower

The Superbird was based on the Roadrunner, but it also had a huge trunk spoiler and a big plastic nose. Both of these features were there for a reason: to make the car more aerodynamic. The Superbird was fast. It could reach speeds of 190 miles (306 km) per hour.

MILESTONES

1963

Chrysler, owner of Plymouth and Dodge, decides to compete with Ford and Chevrolet in NASCAR racing. The company makes the Plymouth Superbird and Dodge Charger for this purpose.

1971

New NASCAR rules about high rear spoilers mean the Superbird can no longer be raced. It is withdrawn from sale.

UNDER THE SKIN

In spite of its different look, the Superbird has the same body and chassis as the Plymouth Roadrunner.

Pontiac GTO

The Pontiac GTO was the first muscle car. It was made from a Pontiac Tempest fitted with parts that made the car more powerful.

Pontiac dealers supplied buyers with GTO badges as part of a special "extras" pack.

GTO stands for "Gran Turismo Omologato," which is Italian for "grand touring racing car." Pontiac copied this phrase from Ferrari, the famous Italian racing car maker.

The GTO was plain to look at. Its body was the same as the regular Pontiac Tempest.

Three body styles were available: a two-door coupe, a four-door coupe, and a two-door convertible, like this one.

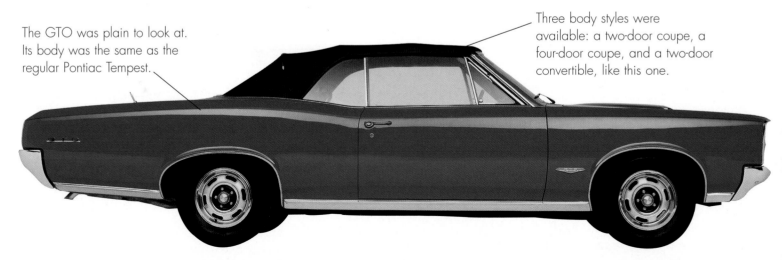

Like many other Pontiacs, the GTO had stacked headlights. The owner of this GTO added "GR-RRR!" in place of the front license plate to show how tough the car is.

If General Motors had its wish, the Pontiac GTO would never have existed. The U.S. government criticized the company for building too many fast and powerful cars that were considered dangerous, especially for young drivers.

First Muscle Car

Pontiac, which is owned by General Motors, found a way around the problem. The company sold "GTO packs" that buyers used to turn a Pontiac Tempest into a high-performance car. So many people bought the GTO packs, the car soon became known as the GTO. In this way, Pontiac created America's first muscle car — and many other car makers soon followed.

MILESTONES

1964

Pontiac offers "GTO Packs" to Tempest buyers. The muscle car is born.

1967

Pontiac itself begins building GTOs and introduces the most powerful model of all. With a 400-cubic-inch (6,554-cc) V-8, it can top 140 miles (225 km) per hour.

UNDER THE SKIN

With a 393-cubic-inch (6,440-cc) V-8 engine, the GTO could reach a top speed of 120 miles (193 km) per hour. This was faster than most cars of its time.

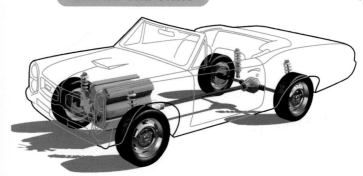

Glossary

accelerate to increase speed

aerodynamic having a smooth, sleek surfaces around which air easily flows

big-block engine a large, powerful engine first built by Chevrolet for their most powerful trucks and cars

chassis the part of a car body to which the engine, transmission, and suspension are attached

coupe a two-door car, usually seating two people

customized having special features added, such as a larger engine, a special suspension, a new paint job, or different wheels

cylinder a chamber inside the engine where a piston is forced up and down by burning gasoline to create power

disc brakes brakes that work by pressing a metal plate against rubber pads to slow the car down

exhaust pipes metal tubes that take the gasses from burned fuel away from an engine and make it quieter

fiberglass a lightweight material made from glass strands and plastic

front-wheel drive a system that sends a car's power from its engine to its front wheels

grille a guard at the front end of the car that lets in air to cool the engine

horsepower a unit of measure of the power of an engine

luxury special and expensive

muscle car an American-made, two-door sports car with a powerful engine for high-performance driving

NASCAR National Association for Stock Car Racing

rollcage a protective frame built into the body of a car

sedan a closed automobile with two or four doors and front and rear seats

shock absorbers devices fitted to a car that give it a smoother ride on bumpy surfaces

sports car a small, high-powered car that usually seats two people

stock car races races between normal production cars that have been altered for greater speed

suspension a system of springs at the base of a car's body that keeps the car even on bumpy surfaces

transmission a system in a vehicle that controls its gears, sending power from the engine to the wheels to make them move

V-8 an engine that has eight cylinders placed opposite each other in a V-shape

vents slits or openings that take in or let out air or fumes

wheel arches parts of the car body that are cut out to allow the wheels to be put on and taken off

For More Information

Books

American Muscle Cars, 1960–1975. Cars & Trucks (series). Bruce LaFontaine (Dover Publications)

Big Book of Cars. (DK Publishing)

Car. DK Eyewitness (series). Richard Sutton and Elizabeth Baquedano (DK Children)

Cars. All About (series). Peter Harrison (Southwater)

Muscle Cars. Automania! (series). Katherine Bailey (Crabtree Publishing Company)

Street Power. Hot Wheels (series). Bill Coulter (Motorbooks International)

The Story of the Ford Mustang. Classic Cars (series). Jim Mezzanotte (Gareth Stevens Publishing)

Web Sites

All Muscle Cars
www.allmusclecars.com

Museum of Automobile History
www.themuseumofautomobilehistory.com

Oldsmobile Toronado
encyclopedia.classicoldsmobile.com/toronado

Publishers note to educators and parents:
Our editors have carefully reviewed these Web sites to ensure that they are suitable for children. Many Web sites change frequently, however, and we cannot guarantee that a site's future contents will continue to meet our high standards of quality and educational value. Be advised that children should be closely supervised whenever they access the Internet.

Index